Taylor's Boomer Humor and Other Useful Poems

by taylor

so what
is this tag? one's
Some gag?
weird I feel
Cause Like a kid
Is
i t
something
I
did ?

Published by B&B&LEE LTD.
taylorsboomerhumor@gmail.com

ISBN: 9781796678888

Library of Congress Control Number: 2019936269

Copyright © 2019 B&B&LEE LTD.

Light of the Moon, Inc. - Publishing Division
Carbondale, Colorado
www.lightofthemooninc.com

I dedicate this book to whomever
will pick it up and read through it.

I hope it brings sun to a rainy day,
happiness to your heart
and helps to enhance your loving
kindness...

INDEX OF CONTENTS

INDEX OF CONTENTS

INDEX OF CONTENTS

INDEX OF CONTENTS

WARNING PAGE

The author of this book, Taylor, has been
diagnosed with PPS,
(Peter Pan Syndrome) by Docker Holdanish,
Minister of Fun Stuff.

The longterm prognosis for Taylor is obvious,
<u>he will never grow up!</u>

Please read these poems with
wonderment and care.

<u>*Do not consume this book in one reading.*</u>

<u>*It is recommended that you
take no more than three poems per day.*</u>

Boomer Humor

There's been a rumor
That I am a boomer
But how could they know
My years surely don't show

I'm still just a boy
Whose mind fills with wonder
Who still finds great joy
Whose heart beats
with thunder

Put some gum in her hair
To show her I care
Skip a stone, hit a ball
I can still do it all

ODE TO A BOOK SHOP

I have a favorite, little Book Shop
When I walk by, my legs they just STOP!

Doors open, they beckon like the cover of a book
I slide inside.... I take a look.

I know I'll find a book to read
One which might just plant a seed.

Inside this cover I'll take a trip,
I'll sail upon a magic ship
To a place I'd never get to go
Or to teach me something I'd never know.

Here, I'll find a book to explore the world
Or one, to be on a couch... all curled.

Yes, this little shop provides for me
A way to sail upon a sea,
A way to let my mind go free,
OOOH, a way to another way to be.

LOVING KINDNESS

cultivate your loving kindness
it's the thing that almost always binds us

plant some here and plant some there
Yes, spread it spread it everywhere

Hair in my Ear......

Oh no! I've now got some hair in my ear
Appears to be more year after year
At first, it seemed so very queer
But, now my whole body's beginning to fear
As youth, which we all hold so dear
Is beginning to just disappear

Is it old age, which is coming more near?
I don't know, cause I find it harder to hear
And my mind is not quite as clear
So my thoughts are beginning to veer

I'm relating my story, so don't shed a tear
I can only tell you, I'm very sincere

But don't be the one who'll laugh and who'll sneer
Cause your time will come, your clock too will shift gear
You'll look in your undies, a brown spot, a smear
Oh no! You've just pooped right out of your rear!

WHERE I WANT TO BE...

IN THE NOW IS WHERE, NOT BEFORE OR NOT AFTER....
TO FILL THIS MOMENT, WITH JOY AND WITH LAUGHTER....

HOW TO HOLD THE NOW TO FILL YOUR MIND....
MAY TAKE YOU A LIFETIME OF TRYING, TO FIND....

WHY SHOULD A TREE LIVE LONGER THAN ME?

Why should a tree live longer than me?
Seems like the way, it's just meant to be.

Well, I've got some skin that keeps me together
And he has his bark, stands up to all weather.

And I've got some hair all over my head
And he has green leaves, turn orange and red.

Well, I can out think him, as smart as I am
And he can just stand there and not give a damn.

So why is he here the day I am born
Still stands among friends,
when for me they do mourn?

Now I can tell you, I do know the reason,
All that I have, is just one long season.

Each time there's a Spring, trees' rebirth you'll see
But when my winter's done, there'll be no more me.

Yes, I am so clever and bright, I can reason
But still can't get more than just one full season.

And as I get older I keep slowing and slowing.
Well, why can't I think of a way to keep going?

So, who is the better in life's awkward plan
For the tree, at my age, I'm becoming a fan.

tree with swing at Anita Witt's Ranch, Carbondale, Colorado

Who's At The Controls

What makes us go up
What makes us come down
One minute a smile
One minute a frown

Our minds take us here
Our minds take us there
Am I at the controls ?
Do we make a good pair?

I don't know which one
is making the choices…
I think it depends
what we're told by our voices.

Guess what I'm NOT ?

Not a fish, an insect or a bird of wing
Four paws I do have, unconditional love is my thing.

I've got floppy ears, and a tail that just wags
If you look from the side, my belly… it sags.

I love to meet babies with food on their face
Does not matter to me, whatever their race.

All kids I do like, a ball they may throw
For me it's just fun, to run to and fro.

Adults talk to me or give a command
Expecting that I will just understand.

Old people they smile, their eyes become bright
They're feeling right now, a child's delight.

I love to go out, I love to just play
Life's all about fun, being straight, trans or gay.

When I express myself, don't fear being bitten
It's poems that I write, surely not pawly written.

EBD

Hark... Father of the House was heard to say...

"What an Exceedingly, Beautiful Day."

From the top of the steeple, for all different people,

Life is sublime, it's a wonderful time.

I wish I could say, we'll all see a day,

When all will be free, to enjoy their own E B D.

MONAStICAL MARMOTS

Our home's on the range by the Monastery
Our lives, so exalted, and always we're merry.

We live in the moment, a life oh so free
Just basking in sun, is where you can find me.

If danger does come, a squeak I give out
My friends, they take cover, their face all a pout.

We lounge and we snack, to fill up our day
We'll do this all summer, till grass turns to hay.

What I Can Not Put Into Words....

Here's my old dog, lies right by my feet.
I look in her eyes, they're all about sweet.

The spirit that binds us, is an unspoken word.
I smile... she grins... although nothing's been heard.

Her head in her paws, over a book I am bent.
It's all about being, together... content.

BROTHERS

Brothers we've been and brothers we are
Our lives were not close, but we've never been far
Lost in an age gap that kept us apart
But forever the other, deep in each heart.

Never knew what it was to have a big brother
Spent his time with his friends or anyone other
A ball and a glove and a bat sometimes too
Would focus his thoughts, it was all he would do

As a brother, I was always just in his way
With me, he did never want to just play
A waste he did call me most of the time
Without me his life was much more sublime

I knew that he loved me, I thought that he did
But how could I tell, being just a small kid
He'd call me some names and slap me around
To be very close, I don't think we were bound

Today I look back and where did life go
For me with my brother I really don't know
Now I am 70 and for him 7 more
Each of our lives filled with what was in store

I love him, I'm happy his life has been grand
I just wish at some time we'd have walked hand and hand
Guess, together our lives have never been much
It's mostly about just keeping in touch

Why has it been this way, no one to blame
If we could do it all over, think I'd just be the same
So why do I feel that we've missed such a lot
For us this worked best, believe it or not…….

written by the father of the bride…

on her wedding day…

A LOVE POEM

Life is a journey, it's one's time, it's one's space.
Some never slow down, some make it a race.

I envy the person, who'll take time, plant a flower,
Then nurture and feed it to give it life's power.

Who'll sit with a chicken and watch that hen lay,
Then ponder that wonder, a miracle that day.

To appreciate life's greatness that comes from above,
To those special people, I wish only love.

What is this thing love, so hard to explain,
A special condition some have in their brain?

If you've found it you'll know, your heart will stay loyal,
But to last a whole lifetime takes hard work and some toil.

Well love, it can come in so many ways,
A person, a thing, a purple mountain haze.

So savor them now all of love's special treasures,
But batten the hatches for all types of weathers.

Together you'll laugh, scream, cuddle and cry,
Your lives will be richer, loves certain high.

Now life will continue in all different ways,
But married you'll be, for the rest of your days.

A Special Moment For Mee...

I saw one, oh now two birds just sitting on a wire
no four oh no six, well now a whole choir.

All facing me squarely, with feathery breast
they sing me a sweet song, they're from many a nest.

I'll remember this gift from my choir on wings
as off they each fly to do other things.

You may think this trite and not worthy a poem
but I'll cherish their song, when I'm far far from home.

Niko....

When he's left at home, I come unlock the door
I hastily enter, and there on the floor...
From a deep sleep he rises, his crate starts to rattle
He knows I will take him, its time to skedaddle...

With his powerful body, coat already on
Like a teenager rising, this dog gives a yawn
Yes, out of this place, he'd rather be
So I unlock his crate and he smiles right at me

Rushes on past, right to the front door
With great expectation, just uses his paw
He's out in bright sunlight, his nose up in the air
Receiving a message, but can't tell from where

"Ah, no one has been here since I was last out"
Double checks the perimeter, with his face in a pout
Done with that job, let's go... anywhere will be fine
You grab the leash, and put me "on line"

More messages coming from every which way
From the air, from the ground, what a beautiful day
His whole body is wagging with the purest delight
He's pulling, he's tugging, "come on... let's take flight"

"To the dog park" I tell him, you'll run and you'll play
Meet all your good friends and have your own way
At the car, before travel, must stop for a tinkle,
Now knows where we're going, his eyes have a twinkle

Yes, this is what good friends are totally for,
To help one another, to enjoy life much more
Whether dog or cat or the whole human race
Go out of your way, bring a smile to a face

NIKO

As I whisper sweet words, your life comes to its end
I'm knowing I'll never have, such another great friend
We bonded together, right from our start
You looked oh so fierce, I knew... you're all heart

Face so expressive with thoughts of your own
I could hear you thinking, "life's just one big bone"
Unconditional love, great strength and great power
Majestically yours, could make any beast cower

Our love oh so great, not like a dog and a man
Understanding each other, as no others can
We'd sniff at the air, not a care on our faces
And off we would go, explored so many places

We didn't let on, how special our time
Our loving and caring, was oh, so sublime
It seems, on those days, the fun that we had
Could only be known, by a boy and a dad

We went through your stages, from pup to a kid
Then through adolescence and onto life's mid
We finally crossed times with both of us grey
And now you've gone on, to the end of your stay

Knowing our bond, was special indeed
Forever in my heart, you've planted your seed
Maybe we'll meet, if there's more time to spend
I'll keep looking for you, after my life's at end

I'm troubled right now, with saying good bye
When I look up above, I see you there in the sky
Happy with friends, or just chewing a toy
Maybe some time again, we'll be a dad and a boy

The Mind's Eyes

Isn't it interesting, what our mind's eyes see
It aways seems different, for you and for me.

For people who look at the same exact thing
For one a necessity, for the other just bling.

Here are some known facts that I'd just ignore
To another who's looking, may make them explore.

To see something scary, that one may take flight
But another may feel, that it looks… oh just right.

Here is a valley, I see beauty, bees hum
To insect and animal it's their life and kingdom.

I see a sun, makes life shine and less bleak
To a farmer with crops, it's rain he may seek.

For each and for all, it's how life comes their way
Make the best as you see it, have a beautiful day.

TATTOOS......

LOTS OF PEOPLE GOT EM..... EVEN ON THEIR
PRIVATES, EVEN ON THEIR BOTTOM.
WHAT IS IT ABOUT LOOKING LIKE ART,
I CONSIDER IT BEING NOT REALLY THAT SMART.
BUT WHO AM I TO ADD MY TWO CENTS,
TO EVERYONE ELSE, I GUESS IT MAKES SENSE.
LOVE, MOM, BIRTH OR SOME DAY,
YES, AS YOU GROW OLDER THEY'LL SIMPLY DECAY.

SOME CAN BE BEAUTIFUL, AN ARTISTIC DELIGHT,
SOME CAN BE POWERFUL, REFLECTING ONE'S MIGHT,
BUT MOST LOOK TO ME, I MEAN THE ONES I CAN SEE
THAT THEY SHOULD JUST HAVE BEEN SPOKEN,
AND THEY'D HAVE SAVED ALL THAT POK'EN!

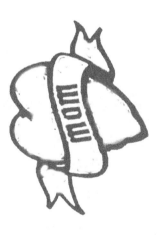

GRAMPYDOM

I know that this baby
has opened my heart,
As life it does play,
I have a new part.

His smile lights my face,
and reminds me anew,
How he can make me forget,
what makes me feel blue.

When I look at his hand,
so small in mine,
His touch brings me wonder,
and makes me feel fine.

His power to heal,
is a mighty thing,
As I think of him now,
makes my heart want to sing.

He looks at me,
with interest galore,
I hope I can help,
in the world he'll explore.

Grampydom yes!
it has sort of a ring,
For me, I can't think of a
much better thing.

Limerick:

A doctor once mixed up a seed

For two people who were in great need

Hoping for joy

Yes, out popped a boy

For them, this was a great deed.

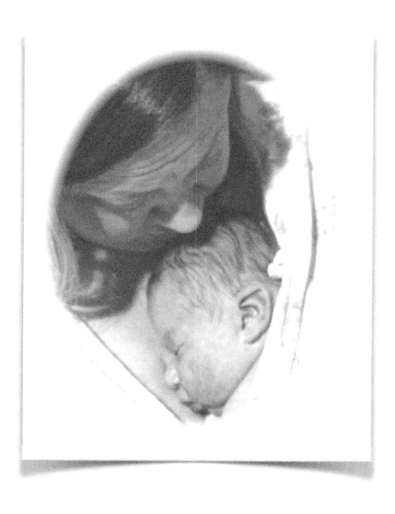

NURSERY RHYME FOR CJ

GOOD MORNING, GOOD MORNING,
OH MISTER CJ
AND WHAT WILL WE DO,
ON THIS MARVELOUS DAY?

IN THE MOUNTAINS WE LIVE, A
HIKE WE CAN TAKE
OR MAYBE JUST SIT BY,
A BEAUTIFUL LAKE....

GOOD MORNING, GOOD MORNING,
OH MISTER CJ
TIME TO GET UP,
YES TIME TO GO PLAY...

EXPLORING WE'LL GO,
THERE'S SO MUCH TO SEE,
JUST ANOTHER GREAT DAY,
FOR YOU AND FOR ME...

YES, ANOTHER GREAT DAY,
FOR YOUR OLD GRAMPY T!

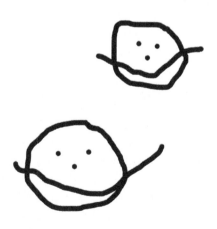

I've Never Met An Ant
That Can't

They'll move a stone without a moan

they'll cut a leaf without a beef

they'll walk a mile and keep a smile

they'll climb a tree, they'll chase a bee

They'll call on their friends when needing a hand

they'll do any chore no matter how grand

some ice-cream has dripped from your cone with a splat

they'll show up as an army, in nothing flat.

They're part of a team, a family you see

who work together much better, than yes, you and me

survival's their game, this is their quest

to continue to live, each depends on the rest.

These guys, they have a wee little brain

but compared to us, seem so much more sane

so who will remain, when humans just can't

I can tell you right now, surely the ant.

Stella, Wonder Dog......

Stella is, a dog of small stature,
although there's no way you really could catch her.

Running and playing and basking in sun,
yes, this is a Stella that's all about fun.

Streaking along, a big grin on her face,
I'm sure she is happy in any old place.

Black and white, and senses so keen,
made to be, a running machine.

Her joy, it is, so easy to see,
no worries, no cares, how we should all be.

Bounding along in sensual delight,
sometimes even airborne, as free as a kite.

She circles again till she has no more,
so happy and pleased right to her core.

Comes along side me, panting and sweet,
I'm oh so surprised as I look at her feet.

Wagging her tail, so full of life,
a lesson to learn, in conquering one's strife,

Making the best, with just legs of three,
<u>hum</u>... how would I do, if Stella were me?

POST ON YOUR REFRIGERATOR DOOR

TEAR HERE++++++++++++++++++
or here+++++++++++++++++++++
<u>RECIPE:</u> Happiness can
sometimes be a choice…
So don't always listen to
your inner voice…
Get joy from giving
whatever you can…
From each gift you'll find
a loving fan…
Be grateful and open your
heart every day…
And you'll surely find
happiness along the way.

++++++++++++++++++++++++++++
and here++++++++++++++++++++++

The Best from the Rest

By adding some years,
must now conquer your fears...
So in this life that you host,
you're getting the most.

Cause what's left from now on,
will quickly be gone.
With much haste and much speed,
so there's surely a need.

To be here in the now,
must learn to know how.
Will help for your rest,
to lead life at its best.

Try to be in the moment,
treasure good things and share...
Take each day at hand,
live with hope and some dare.

For things that are bad,
or you just do not favor.
Exclude them each day,
try some other flavor.

And leave your baggage behind,
and you will see you may find...
You'll live your life with more zest,
and get the Best from the Rest!

Fearful Flowers

Ladened with pollen, standing tall to the sun,

But where are our friends, we see not a one ?

That buzzing symphony, life's music to hear,

There is none at all, should we now have great fear ?

To carry our precious gift on its way,

Who'll pollinate grass, flowers and hay ?

How will the colors from Nature's bouquets

Continue to flourish on life's future days ?

Good Thoughts

There once was a boy,
felt no happiness, none!
See, in his short life,
he had never had fun.

He walked with his chin
buried deep in his chest
And he never looked up
to see life at its best.

Never felt pride
in the work that he did
And never showed joy
on his face as a kid.

One day on his travels
he looked up and down
In the expressions of people,
he saw not a frown.

He thought and he thought
how he felt about life
And realized that others
were filled with more strife.

He asked, "why am I down
in the dumps every day?
Why not live my life
in some better way?"

He felt that he could
and cracked his first smile
To appreciate life,
yes, it took him a while.

What makes his life now
much more happy and gay?
He uses only good thoughts
to fill his whole day.

For me this has worked,
yes, time and again
Maybe that's why I've written
it down with my pen.

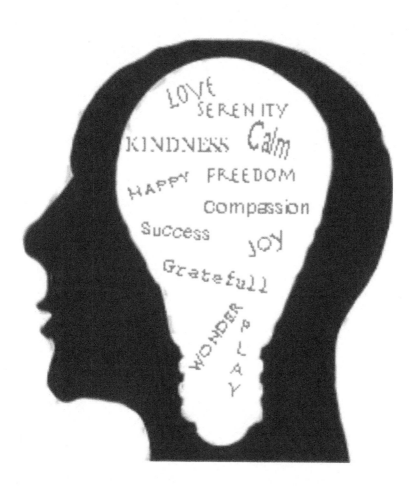

Limerick For David......

Well, how do you measure a man...
It is something I don't think you can...

Just summarize his joys.
And count up his toys.

And remain all your days as his fan...

Cat Tale !

I am a very little cat,
I have a simple brain.

It's just this thing
that follows me,
My tail, I can not
train.

It darts and bobs
and teases me,
Can never just stay plain.

If you ask me why it's doing that,
I really can't explain !

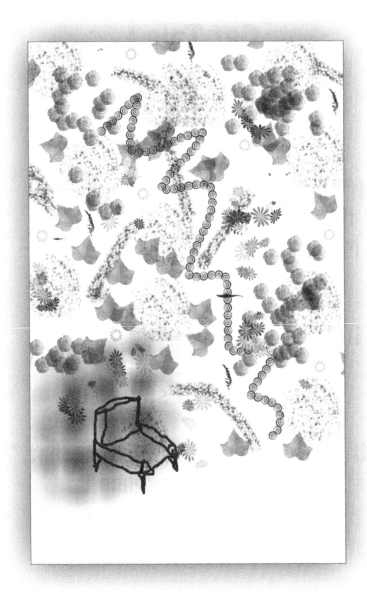

SPOTS,SPO TS,SPOTS

■ ■ ■ ■ ■ ■ ■ ■ ■ ■

SPOTS, SPOTS, SPOTS....
THEY'RE SURELY ARE LOTS.

They're walking right by on the side of that dog.
There's one in the toilet, creating a clog.

There's one on the wall, inside the house.
Bend down and look in,
you can see there's a mouse!

Going to sleep, they're all in your head.
Open your eyes now, ***they're right in your bed!***

Look in your milk, there's always one there.
On Aunt Mabel's chest, there's one with a *hair!*

Or a spot can be, just a place, you see.
Or a spot can be, made for just you and for me.

A spot that is mine, is right here in this chair.
When my butt is upon it, I have not a care!

....

TIME

Time is on your side, so they say
However, it's the only thing you cannot delay

You can put off a meal to eat, or alter a date to meet
Extend your time to go, or even just take it slow

But, you cannot play with the time of day
See time is the ration of life's celebration

So what is this time that we have in our life?
A chance to do good, a chance to bring strife?

We each choose a path, must encounter the wrath
Of the course that we've laid, in the life that we've made

So help all or help one, or just help yourself
I've found the former to be of great wealth

You get just one chance, for your life to enhance
Your wonderful stay, in this world everyday

And once it is gone, it will not return
No matter how much, you wish and you yearn

So cherish it all, moments big, moments small
For tomorrow you see, may be no you or me

Shrimp
Tale

How come shrimp, come dressed only in tails
On pasta or salads, it just never fails.

I'd like to get a shrimp cocktail one day,
Without any tails, yes, to have it my way.

I can't remove them without making a mess,
Or just chopping them off, then to eat I have less.

It doesn't really tell me, if it's fresh from the sea,
I think they leave it on, just to hassle me!

I really don't think the shrimps give a dam,
Can you remove them for me please?

*And I'll be as happy
as this clam....*

Testimonial to a Food that is Underappreciated.....an edipoem

Pinwheels, a food that really is grand

Be careful, make haste, or they'll melt in your hand.

With chocolate, it's covered and marshmallow too

Will clear up what ails you, even if you are blue.

I melt them, I freeze them, they're good any way

Can eat them at night or have them all day.

I gobble them down, with oh so much joy

Been doing it since, I was just a small boy

And if you want a good healthy meal

Just try some veggies, with your next pin-wheel.

But... some people, they say, I eat like a dunce

However, remember, we live only once!

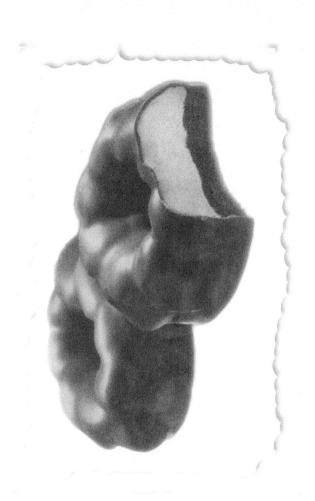

"A Tribute to Shel Silverstein"

Shel writes of sharing, in his *The Giving Tree*
I write of life, what it means to me

Now I have time to appreciate
What life has laid, upon my plate

And giving and sharing are two great things
To help one fulfill, all that life brings

So having, you see, goes more than one way
Or you can live your whole life, as a lonely stay

CATTYWAMPUS

DID YOU KNOW THAT
<u>CATTYWAMPUS</u> IS A WORD?
WHILE SPEAKING WITH FRIENDS,
T'WAS ALL THAT I HEARD!

WRITE A LETTER, YOU CAN SPELL IT
MORE THAN ONE WAY.
OR TRY TO PLACE IT INTO A SENTENCE
THAT ANYONE CAN SAY.

BUT, IF YOU CAN PROPERLY USE
<u>CATTYWAMPUS</u>...
PLEASE, PLEASE, PLEASE, OH PLEASE...
DON'T BE OH SO POMPOUS.

A Snake.....

I see a snake
He's by the lake
A big big deal, I will not make

My mom sez, careful snakes may bite
But only if I provoke the fight

Could be a moccasin, could be a viper
Both of those snake can make you get hyper

I'd like him for a pet, you see
I think he'd fall in love with me

I'll catch him now, a piece of cake
He's heading right back to the lake

I'm getting closer, there he goes
Oops, he's just a garden hose!

Whomever.....

To me Mother Nature, others have their own name
However you say it, the meaning's the same
From her you see, you can not make a demand
Cause in every instance, she'll play her own hand.

Destruction can be the card that she plays
Or bathe us in soft and warm sun shiny rays.
She likes to surprise, whenever she pleases
But in Spring and in Fall, I'm ladened with sneezes.

She's most incredible when right on her game
When she's not showing her fury and not seeking fame.
When she fills our space with colors galore
With rainbows and flower and oh so much more.

I thank her each day, for the presents she brings
Fills my heart just to hear, a bird when he sings
The air oh so fresh, the sky when it's blue
Life's simple pleasures, and it's all free to you!

A Difference?

Where did the time go, it really does fly
Seems like its past, in the wink of an eye.

When Mick he did sing, "time's on our side"
At 20, could not imagine, how fast was the ride.

Is there a difference, because of my stay
Had serious times, but most of it play.

Got hitched with my lady, through life we did blaze
Hey, with 50 behind us, was not just a phase.

A child we had, and at times we did stumble
When together, our lives were sometimes a rumble.

I look where I'm at, yes the big 7-oh!
Is there a difference I've made? I really hope so.

Intending through life, that I never did miss
Any chance that I had, to spread happiness, bliss.

I think there are many good things that I've done I
hope to some lives, I've brought happiness, sun.

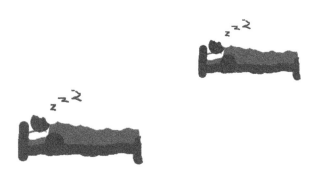
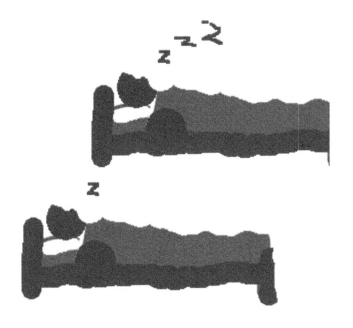

NAP TIME....

When I was young, a snooze I'd not take
It seemed so important to just be awake

Throughout all my life, I was a typical type-A
Busy working and planning for the very next day

Now I'm much older, far down the trail of life's map
Not a day does go by, I don't treasure my nap.

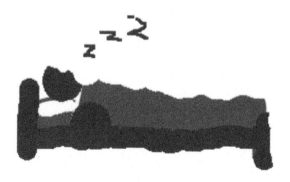

Snores in the Room

I have a very happy life…
See at home, it's just me and my wife.

Living with us now, our granddog too.
He helps me through, the times that I'm blue.

I was sleeping last night and heard noises galore.
I knew not from where, then I looked towards the floor.

And there was the granddog moving his paws.
And out from his nose came these loud hardy snores.

I think he was chasing some dogs in his dreams.
Running and playing and jumping in streams.

He starts to awake and looks into my eyes.
Sees he's still in his bed, to his great surprise.

Looks all around, comes a smile to his face.
Now knows he's at home, where he's safe in this place.

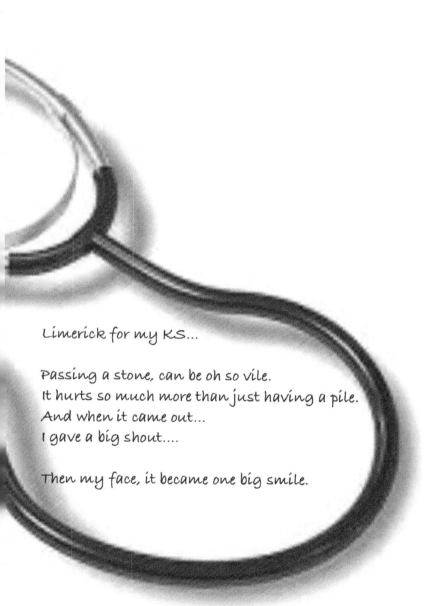

Limerick for my KS...

Passing a stone, can be oh so vile.
It hurts so much more than just having a pile.
And when it came out...
I gave a big shout....

Then my face, it became one big smile.

If I....

If I wasn't this person,
would there be me?

If I wasn't a person,
what would I be?

If I was something else,
would I understand how?

If I was this else,
could I be thinking this now......

a poem?

... a limerick for Brother Martin

"BRO"

Today, I was called "BRO" by another,
but for us there is no common mother.

Yes, ordained this man was,
it's religion he does....

Guess now I'm the "bro" of a Brother.

Continuum·················

I don't think, I'd like
to die in the cold.
Be there so stiff,
and a sight to behold.

I don't think, I'd like
to die where its hot.
Especially not,
in some savage's pot.

I don't think, I'd like
to die where its warm.
Definitely not,
by some bees in a swarm.

I don't think, I'd like
a way that is cool.
Not over a woman,
or shot in a duel.

I don't think the weather
will ever be right.
So, I'll keep trying to avoid
my very last plight.

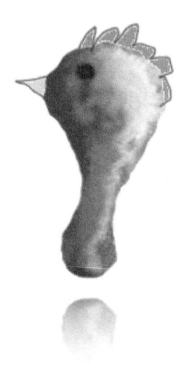

ODE TO FRIED CHICKEN .....

I had a big helping of fried chicken today,
And I realized, from the blue, to my total dismay.

It's the fried stuff I like, oh so much more,
The chicken in fact, is a terrible bore.

For all of my life, fried chicken's been a wonderful treat,
And now I am realizing, it's not been the meat.

It's crispy and greasy... to have it made for just you,
Tell the chef, hold the chicken, it's the crust that will do.

If you see a sign at a restaurant door,
"All the fried chicken you can eat!"... to you I implore....

That you do not stop in, cause you'll only want more,
And you'll eat all the crispies, then walk out the door.

It's the chicken you'll leave in big heaps and big piles,
With your belly so stuffed and your face full with smiles.

So to get it just right, when ordering this food
Speak slowly and clearly, but do not be rude,

"So, I'll have a serving of fried chicken skin,"

......It's the way that your order, should always begin.

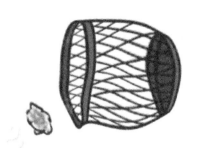

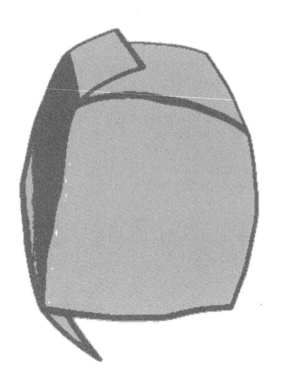

Born With Instructions :

How would you do, if you already knew,
How long from your birth, till you're gone from this Earth?

Born with instructions, that clearly read...
"How to keep clean" Oh, and "when you'll be dead"

Would you put a note in some obscure place?
Or show it with fear every day on your face?
Be grateful for all that you've learned and you've done?
Or be sad you might miss some really great fun?

Don't worry and worry comes closer that day,
Or you'll wish and you'll hope your whole life away!

Appreciate now what you have and can do,
See, tomorrow's the day there may not be you!

I'm so glad I don't know the day I'll be past,
I look forward to each, sure it won't be my last.

Dogs Set the Best Example

I think dogs have become,
the ultimate people...
In my mind, they've made it,
to the top of the steeple.

While dogs in the park,
seem to work it all out.
When humans converge now,
they push and they shout,

While, dogs defecate in the dirt,
we defecate on each other,
But their's feeds the earth,
while our's hurts a brother.

And unconditional love,
 you can get from a mutt,
So… if you want a better world,
start by sniffing a butt?

SMELL THE ROSES

People who can smell the roses
Don't necessarily have special noses

They do however take the time
To find what makes the world sublime

They can find it here, they can find it there
They can find it almost anywhere

Some people call it state of mind
It's really not so hard to find

So before you reach your end called death
Stop a moment and take a breath

You too can see what life's about
But not by burying your face, in a pout

You may surprise yourself and see
There's more out there for you and me

Don't miss it all, it's not too late
Just take life's joys to fill your plate

PLAYGROUNDING....

I went to the playground with my grandson today
We were merrily, merrily engrossed in our play.

Along came a mother with her daughter in tow
She said, while looking it's easy to know…

… that boy you are with will never need a brother
… the two of you are so lucky, to have one another.

SEESOARERS

Spider On The Wall !!!!!

There is a spider upon the wall,
While I sit inside this bathroom stall.

He runs along
Must do his job
Catching bugs
He's quite a slob!

I tell myself
I fear him not
Don't come too close
You little dot!

He really does not come so near
I cannot understand my fear
He runs along on legs of eight
I see MYSELF upon his plate!

Let him live, he's nature's best
But please don't land upon my chest!
I'll let you be, don't come once more
Or I'll have to protect with strength and gore!

I turn my head, myself to clean
He's disappeared! He is so mean!

Autumn Rush

The water runs free
Just beyond my knee
I can clearly see
The water runs free

It really does tumble
Along with a rumble
It's the only sound
So very profound

There's autumn's leaf
Which falls to this thief
And away it goes
Where nobody knows

Takes a bobble, a dip
On its faraway trip
So brave and so bold
On this ribbon of cold

This river runs free
That's how I want to be

B S

One of the great joys in life
Can be rendered in bed by a loving wife

It can feel so good, it can make you giggle
If she really gets into it, adds a wiggle

Thoughts in your head, fantasies galore
If you're really hard up, use the edge of a door

Or improvise now, there are so many ways
To feel this great pleasure, for days after days

If your quest is fulfilled, you have found that spot
If you do, oh, you'll want a lot, yes a lot

Back scratching, I can tell you is always such bliss
One of life's pleasures, be sure not to miss!

WORRY

OH, I'VE GOT THAT GENE
FOR WHICH THERE IS NO TOXIC SCREEN
IT CAN MAKE YOU LOSE WEIGHT, YES MAKE YOU LEAN
IT CAN EVEN GRAB HOLD AND MAKE YOU MEAN.

IT COMES INTO MY MIND, OCCUPIES THE SPACE
WITHOUT AN INVITE, IT MAKES IT RACE
I DO NOT WANT IT IN THIS PLACE
SOMETIMES IT CREEPS UPON MY FACE.

I CAN STAY UP ALL NIGHT
WITH A TERRIBLE FRIGHT
NO MATTER HOW MUCH I FIGHT AND I FIGHT
THESE THOUGHTS THEY HANG ON WITH ALL THEIR MIGHT

WHY DO YOU THINK IT WANTS INTO MY MIND?
IT'S THOUGHTS OF THIS KIND I'D RATHER NOT FIND
SO HELP ME PLEASE! PLEASE HELP ME, PUT THEM BEHIND
NATURE'S WAY OF BEING UNKIND?

IT MAY BE THIS WORRY THAT MAKES COWS MOO...
OR EVEN SOME DIRTY STREET PIDGONS COO...
THESE FEELINGS OF WORRY CAN MAKE ME SO BLUE...
OH NO!! IS IT SOMETHING THAT YOU HAVE TOO!!

The Scientific Study:
The Four Most Important
Properties of Chocolate:

an edipoem

CHOCOLATE

When you have it warm, it's sweet and gooey.

At room temperature, it's soft and chewy.

If you have it cold, it's hard but creamy.

But, best of all.... **IT MAKES ME DREAMY!**

A FACT

I love my life and
I love my wife
And side by side
It's been an incredible ride
Cause the love that we have
is greater then time
Without it our lives
would be far less sublime

On the occasion of our anniversary...

Roses are Red
Violets are Blue
Another Year Together
The More I Love You

"EARTH"...abstracted from a work by
Marcel Majid Kahhak, artist extraordinaire.

114

Why Am i Here In This Place?

Why am i here in this place?
Surrounded by beauty and grace

Why this spot on the Earth?
Not close to my place of birth

Is it chance that has landed me here?
I don't think that will ever be clear

Is it part of some great master plan?
Think it's more than just fate for this man

Why am i here in this place?
Guess it's just my kind of space

There's A Certain Feeling

There's something you can feel, deep down inside
Not on the surface, but beyond one's thick hide.

Some people get it, and some people don't
Some people want it, and some people won't.

I for one, thrive on this feeling
Keeps me sober and strong, and it helps me with healing.

It's the feeling of being… loved by another,
A feeling that should start, first with one's mother.

It's the feeling that keeps my furnace a'roaring
It's a feeling that keeps my heart's beat a'soaring.

It can open your eyes, let the sunshine stream in,
It's a feeling to make each day begin.

If you can't find it now, you may be feeling the blues
So search in your heart, sure to find clues.

Yes, love is the thing, makes my world go round
Without it, my life would be much less profound!

Some Bad People Can Change (But Not Always)

Take a new look, at some people you know,
For their change that is good, let some bad feelings go.

In this life's presence, take on this dare,
But, don't give that one person, too big of a share.

Let time mellow out, the way that you think,
Let loving and giving, keep you in the pink.

Find the bad that you feel, and make it not be,
But the best that there is, make that what you see.

Don't seek out the worst, being so judgmental,
Find understanding, be happy, and try to be gentle.

For this, you will see, that you will feel better,
Lift that weight of distraction, may be only a header.

Make good vibes, the thing that you now try to send,
You may be surprised.... find a really good friend!

Courage.....

That fly inside my window,
    he wants his release.

Drawn to the sun,
    his efforts won't cease.

He'll keep trying and trying
    with all of his will.

But by morning he'll be there
    dead on the sill.

Why am I bothered
    this story so trite?

Got no credit for courage
    and the way he did fight!

ON THIS CLEAR WINTER'S DAY

On this clear winter's day
Holding all thoughts at bay

Under sky that's so blue
Painter's pallet, by who?

The trees have their green
Helping air become clean

So white is the snow
This just adds to the show

Like glitter, some ice
Gives a sparkle, so nice

The sun peers from high
Far away in the sky
And its light and its heat
Make *this* day complete

I'll continue along,
Not a sound, nature's song

Hope I'll never be done,
Yes, alive is so fun!

BULL-y-ing is being COW-ard-ly

Cause I'm different from the rest of the herd,
Friends might choose to be mean, there's an unspoken word.

They're not people and so all are utterly kind,
With some boys and some girls that's not easy to find.

But with no mirror to see, the different colors I wear
And no others around, who'll whisper and stare.

Not being human, can be more humane
Cause it's obvious sometimes, being human is lame.

So maybe its easier, to be just a cow.
Or even a cat, I'll just roll over...... meow.

For Mrs Moylan, My Third Grade Teacher, Because I'd Like Her To Know.......

I've written this poem,
inspired by a teacher.
To me an old women,
but for learning, a preacher.

She loved to teach
and to plant all her seeds.
So we'd learn early in life,
to meet most of our needs.

Kindness and loving
she spread through the class.
Was like sitting in church,
during a mass.

Taught us it all, yes...
even hold open that door.
Teachers like her...
they don't make 'em no more.

She liked me I know,
not so different you see.
For in the third grade,
I was all about me.

Yes, I regret...
that she never did know.
That the seeds that she
planted, really did grow.

This poem that I wrote,
in my life in its lateness.
Has proven to be,
a sign of HER greatness.

Now, I really do yearn,
cause I owe her this rhyme.
That she truly would know,
was not wasting her time.

WHAT IF WATER RAN UPHILL?

IF WATER WAS TO RUN UPHILL,
YOU'D NEVER HAVE TO MOP A SPILL.

OUR STREAMS WOULD RUN RIGHT TO THE TOP,
LITTLE DROPS WOULD NEVER PLOP-PLOP-PLOP.

RAIN WOULD FALL UP FROM THE GROUND,
AND YOU'D NEVER HEAR THAT SO-N-SO DROWNED.

YOU WOULD NOT SEE A WATER FALL,
AND YOUR SHOWER WOULD RUN, STRAIGHT UP THE STALL.

YOUR GLASS TO FILL, YOU'D HOLD SO HIGH,
MISS A DROP, LOOK OUT, GOES STRAIGHT TO THE SKY!

IN THE MORNING WHAT A SILLY SIGHT,
YOUR JUICE, IT POURS TO AN AWESOME HEIGHT...
COOKIES AND MILK TO DRINK AT NIGHT,
COULD BE OH, SUCH A TERRIBLE FRIGHT.

IT'S GOOD THAT WATER FLOWS DOWNHILL,
MUCH EASIER TO TAKE A PILL...
OR CLEAN YOURSELF, OR FLUSH THE TOILET,
OR EVEN IN COOKING, JUST TO BOIL IT.

SO, IF YOU EVER SEE A STREAM THAT FLOWS UP,
DON'T EVEN TRY TO FILL YOUR CUP...
CAUSE YOU WON'T BE ABLE TO SWALLOW A DROP,
UNLESS OF COURSE.... YOUR FEET ARE ON TOP!

The <u>Voice</u> and the <u>Sexaphone</u>......

These instruments heard, we know them by name,
From the voice, from the sax, they have garnered great fame.

The lady she stands, how simply she sings,
Her voice is released and comes upon wings.

The man holds his horn, and kisses its lips,
While blowing and stroking, with cool finger tips.

That voice that we hear is perfectly honed,
And married with horn, melodically toned.

The man he caresses and fondles that horn,
His music we hear, it's almost like porn.

Its timbre and tones fill the air oh so sweet,
I'm being massaged, I'm feeling its heat.

They compliment each other, their sound rings so true,
They play with my feelings, from happy to blue.

Their sensuous stories, to the listener are sent,
For me, on this night, I'm much more content.

for Stacey and Jim

Going Home

Today's work, it is done, I head home for the night
But on my way home, its traffic I fight.

As soon as I move, I see a red light
Not a green do I get, it's a terrible fright.

My speed never gets to a reasonable height
I wish I could fly, just like a kite.

There's no reason to try to show off my might
It would just add annoyance and hinder my plight.

The traffic is crazy, the cars are so tight
Oh, city sprawl, you're a terrible blight.

Maybe right here I'll just make a right
And hope that my sweet home will soon be in my sight.

WHEN I WAS A KID, THEY CALLED IT "THAT THING"...

IF YOU CAME TO THIS WORLD EQUIPT AS A BOY,
BY NOW YOU MUST KNOW, YOU'VE BEEN BLESSED WITH A TOY.

YOU MAY HAVE BEEN TOLD BY THE CHURCH, OR YOUR MOM.
IF YOU TOUCH IT AT NIGHT, MAY GO OFF LIKE A BOMB.

OR, DON'T PLAY WITH "THAT THING," UNDER YOUR SHORTS,
OR YOUR HANDS WILL DISPLAY ALL SORTS OF WARTS.

SON, LEAVE "THAT" ALONE!... THAT MOTHER JUST SAID,
AND THE BOY LOOKED UP WITH HIS FACE A BRIGHT RED.

NOW I KNOW YOU WOULD LOVE TO BE ABLE TO FLY
TO BE ABLE TO SOAR ALL AROUND IN THE SKY.

BUT THIS "THING" THAT BOYS HAVE, YES ONE OF "THOSE THINGS,"
SOME DAY YOU WILL REALIZE, IT'S BETTER THAN WINGS.

Tulips, too ......

Two lips are better than one,
Otherwise kissing would not be such fun.

One lip would just hang,
and you'd never have sang,
and others would giggle,
as your mouth did its wiggle.

But.... to give a bouquet, to a loved one like mother, **Surrrely**, Tulips might work, as well as an-other.

THE BEAST THAT ATE BEES

There once was a beast
Who loved to just feast
On air buzzing bees
Or fur buried fleas.

The bees he would catch
By snapping his jaw
Or slapping his paw
Knocking bees to the floor.

While fleas he would gnaw
Or scratch with one paw
They'd march from his coat
Oops, then right down his throat.

Now why would he eat
such a food with no meat?
And it can't be the flavor
There's nothing to savor.

But bees have their buzz
And fleas hide in fuzz
And both are annoy-in
So he wants to destory-em.

He's really a big gentle kind of a beast
To look at you'd not be afraid in the least.
You'd think he might just want to take it real slow
But oh, it's those bees and those fleas, they really must go!

Horse-fly...

I swatted a horse-fly
who sat on my arm.
It was my blood that he wanted,
not to do me great harm.

Well, sharing with bugs
is just not my thing.
So I raised up my hand
and he then took to wing.

I have plenty of blood,
so sharing seems right.
But this little guy's
got a terrible bite.

I know he would like it,
my blood runs so rich.
But I would wind up
with one hell of an itch!

Yesterday

To some friends I

said something...

that I knew I'd

regret.

Now

I'm hoping and

wishing...

that it's soon they'll

forget.

WORDS

At one time, what we read, t'was beauty on a page,
But now what we read, is about violence and rage.

Upon written word, you could travel and learn,
Be anyone, or simply make your heart yearn.

And why comes this change, and who do we blame,
For the words look alike, but now used to defame.

What was easy to decipher, has become simply extreme,
Now everyone's angry, with a grudge it would seem.

I'd like to return, whence we used a kind word,
Where happiness and goodness, were the things that we heard.

My First Tractor Ride

The key is right here,
it's in the ignition,
This must be a dream,
cause I've always been wish'in.

A ride on a tractor,
a Farmall at that,
Just get her in gear
and away like a bat.

Cruis'in the fields,
sit'in high in her seat,
Wide open spaces,
this is surely, so neat.

Mov'in that cattle
and bail'in that hay,
Out in those fields,
till the last of sun's ray.

Guess being a ranch boy...
since I'm from the city,
It looks kind'a cool,
like the real nitty-gritty.

Now maybe a ranch
is where I should'a been born,
And, I love this old tractor...

but where is the horn**?**

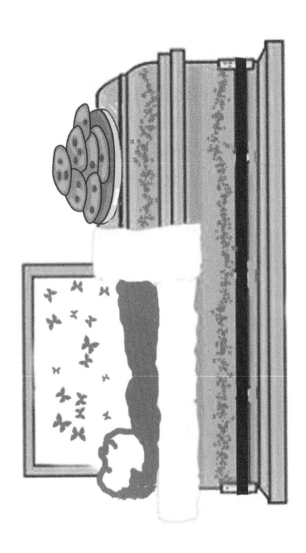

TO HAVE A PLEASANT SLEEP

It's not very often, you get to choose your own coffin.
So do plan ahead, for that very last bed.

Now, I'll take some time, to find one that's comfy
Don't want one that's hard, or even that's lumpy.

I'd like to know now, when I lie there a sleep'n,
They'll be no big bugs, a'crawling and creep'n.

Well, there may not be room, for any more nookie,
But please, please, please, please.... A CHOCOLATE CHIP COOKIE!

My Grandson, Cameron James

I have a new grandson,
I call him CJ
I love to just watch him,
nap, eat and play.

Almost never a tear,
a pout or a cry
He always seems happy,
especially when dry.

I think he's a miracle,
and oh such a pleasure
For all in his future,
I'm sure a great treasure.

Makes me proud and elated,
I'd like you to meet
But most important of all,
this boy... he's so sweet.

To love and to cherish him,
makes me feel so sublime
I hope I am gifted,
with lots more of this time.

Grampy to Three.....

  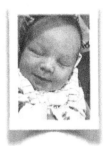

This time that has come,
now grandfather to three
I will strive every day,
so that proud they will be.

One a young lady,
trying to find her own way
I do tell her I care,
in all that I say.

One now a teen,
into sports and a scholar
Our relationship is...
so confused I could holler.

And here we go now,
a new infant, a delight
To love him is easy,
yes with all of my might.

I love each of them,
in their own special way
I'm grateful, I'm thankful,
for every day.

THAT MOOOVELOUS FEELING

Summering in a field, brings the best times to my life,
The grass, there's a plenty, no hunger, no strife.

I can eat all day, gaining so many pounds,
My eating from hunger, it has oh no bounds.

The birds I hear singing, my buddies they moo,
It's about being present, and not feeling blue.

Once in a while, my skin it will twitch,
Oh no, my worst worry, I now have an itch...

To a fence post, a tree or a low hanging branch,
I must get up real close, for what looks like a dance.

So, if you see me one day rubbing some rocks in a pile,
On my face you may find, a big happy smile.

See, it's hard for a cow to scratch any old place,
When I get it just right, it reflects on my face.

Dead Meat

Dead Meat, Dead Meat
Just add some heat
And call it a meal
But, don't hear the pig squeal

Dead Meat, Dead Meat
Just add some heat
And eat it right down
Don't see the cow frown

I'm eating dead meat
Or just some pigs feet
I can try out the spleen
Or bacon cut by machine

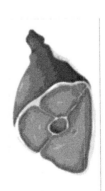

Dead Meat, Dead Meat
Just add some heat
Invite the friends
Another life ends

I can eat the heart
Or the brain to be smart
Now, review what I ate
To regurgitate

Maroon Bells (aspen, colorado)

Maroon is your name
Raw nature your game
Your incredible power
Makes mortal men cower

Lets beauty abound
Around and around
Wherever I look
Every cranny and nook

Nature's gift to us all
Winter, summer, spring, fall
Each season a wonder
Watch out for man's plunder

Now embracing fall snow
To climax the show
Comes winter's sleep
You'll hear not a peep

Have to feel no walkers
And face no gawkers
Hide your presents for now
Come spring again, wow

Then melt will the snow
And on with your show
Can't really blame
Your incredible fame

Nature's beauty is free
It inspires me

INDEPENDENCE PASS, (ASPEN, COLORADO)

INDEPENDENCE, YOUR GRANDEUR WAS CARVED LONG AGO
FROM NATURE A GIFT, A SPECTACULAR SHOW
YOU WAKE NOW FROM SHELTERING SNOW'S WINTER SLEEP
FOR US IT'S A PASSAGE, YOUR BEAUTY TO REAP

SUCH BEAUTY DEFUSED BY DAWN'S EARLY LIGHT
WHEREVER WE LOOK, AN INCREDIBLE SIGHT
YOUR POWER AND RAPTURE SEEPS INTO ONE'S MIND
WILL NEVER FORGET YOU, A FRIEND HARD TO FIND

Life (the beginning)

Life is our time to bloom
Starts within birth mother's womb

In our crib we lie and stare
What lies ahead may not be fair

We'll hear mom's voice from outer space
A smile will form upon my face

Another sound from down the hall
I think I'll try to start to crawl

Our senses they sharpen, we get to our feet
Now walking and talking, the world we will greet

As kids we're meant to be carefree and gay
Our focus on life revolves around play

As we get older we try to mature
Which is not quite so fun as the time just before

We reach and pull, to cut the cord
Without really knowing, to what we look forward

We're at a point, think we know it all
We bounce along, we take a fall

Realizing our lives can be many things
Realizing it's time to take to our wings

We soar through the air with the greatest of ease
Not knowing what direction, not knowing who to please

It's time to go, we leave the nest
"One big step" for meeting life's test

Leon and Sylvia

FOR SYLVIA

Sylvia was one hell of a mother
For children she had just me and my brother

Made us a home so neat and so stable
There when we needed and filled dinner table

Yes, we were lucky as children did go
Her love was unbridled, affection she'd show

It now seems so simple, the life we did lead
To a child while growing, it's everyone's need

EACHDAY…

A day is just a page in each life.

Can bring happiness, memories,
hardship or strife.

Each must endure what
comes their own way.

To continue to live
on this Earth every day.

So, enjoy each one to it's
fullest extent.

It's all precious time,

It's the way we pay rent.

How others see me...

There's a picture of me
that I can not see
It's how others interpret my
words and my motion
Transcribing my thoughts
computing my quotient
It's a picture of me
that I can not see
Not always using
the very right word
Not always how I
mean to be heard

A picture of me
I can not see
Or is it I choose
a certain way
To cast a dispersion
in what I say
A picture of me
Now I see

Fisherman

(for Sandy, on the occasion of his 60th birthday)

This man, he casts with a motion,
slight wrist.
The fly on his line to a spot,
never missed.

A fish near the surface,
he circles to look.
The man on the shore,
gets ready his hook.

Cat and mouse is the game
played by these two.
The fish and the man,
what will each do?

I've got him!
The fisherman reels in his line.
Won't hurt him you know,
cause life's too sublime

"Catch and release,"
they all say it's so fair.
Broke his jaw, poked his eye,
swims away with a scare!

Yes, we are the smartest
of all of God's species.
But sometimes we act
like our brains are pure feces.

Camping Near Rapids

Roaring rapids, you love to show us your white
Tumultuous power, can be an onlooker's fright

More pounding, more thrusting, your bounds become tight
Boiling and churning, your unbridled might

Rumbling, rising all through the night
From rock, from stone, you will carve, you will bite

In morning your silver reflects early light
A true gift of nature, a beautiful sight

To Learn How To Live

I'm thankful almost every day
for this world in which I have time to play

I take a deep breath and wow I get high
I open my eyes from the ground to the sky

there's so much here, use all your senses
approach without fear, let go your defenses

and love will pour in
and you will begin
to learn how to give
to learn how to   !

Chi-dult.....

For me to be an adult one day, I can not perceive,
Cause there's a child inside me, who's not ready to leave.

I've adjusted to age, now it's only a number,
But, I think it has made me, oh so much more humbler.

Yes, I've mellowed with time, but I'm still in my prime.
And the childish things, still put wind in my wings.

So, maybe someday I'll try and be an adult,
However, it might have to be... some type of cult.

Not young.... But not old

I'm not young... but not old
States this man, oh so bold
Hashmarks show me the score
Makes my body feel sore

As time takes its toll
I'll depend on my soul
To keep my mind clear
Of age I may fear

I'll run down my clock
Without taking stock
Of the time that I've spent
And where it all went

For I do have the knack
Keep my train on the track
Final station you see
Will not hinder me

Summers' Passing:

Mother Nature continues life's cycle, new season
But fall's most important, I'll tell you the reason...

So listen real close, cause it's obvious that
Year after year, it's all about scat!

That's right, winter's comm'en, the bears their a bumm'en
The air it be chill'en, bears need to be fili'en
Cause stomach inflation, means good hibernation

Yes, bears sense it too, that fall is in view
They'll come right through your door, and scratch up your floor
But once in your kitchen, they're totally itching
Talk about brazen, every lid they'll be raz'en

It's sweets they love best, they'd leave all the rest
Cakes, cookies and candies, yum, yes they're all dandies
Gone right down their throats, brings a shine to their coats
Bears leave a big mess, they couldn't care less

So watch out this fall, for bears, they don't call
They'll just enter your place, with a smile on their face
And when you get home they'll leave in a hurry
You might even hear their noise as they scurry

Look around at the mess, your mind it will wonder
Has my home been hit by lightning and thunder?

Then go to your bedroom, a gift, what is that?
Oh no! Where you sleep, steaming piles of scat!!!

The Renata Sonata

I cannot hear what's being said
There are no noises in my head
No sound, no note not even clef
You see at hearing, I am stone deaf.

I used to be a gregarious one
And laugh and sing and be included in fun
But now, a wall has arisen, you see
It's a wall that seems to surround only me

I've had to search the universe
To find a different type of verse
To see or taste or touch or smell
One to relieve me from silent hell

And here it is, I've found my place
Surrounded by Nature's incredible grace
Breathtaking beauty resounds in my head
I feel almost fulfilled, natural beauty
instead.

The Day Spent...

I spent my day
In an awesome way
In an awesome place
At an awesome pace

Now it's "kick back" time
And that's real fine
So I'll end this day
In this special way...

Bunnies

Life can be funny
For each different bunny

Some never stop
OOPs, some can not hop

Some run so free
But others can't see

And some show no fear
While others can't hear

He is so fast, he's never late
She has trouble, just thinking straight

So, which little bunny would you rather be?
Can't hear, always late or totally free?
There's really no choice for you and for me.

The world is a place full of all types of bunnies
Can't choose or can't pick, regardless of monies

So hop as you can
Again and again

Be proud of yourself
With your own human wealth

And just be a bunny who others respect
Cause we all know the world's not close to perfect

Bunnies Too

Life can be funny
For each different bunny

Some never stop
OOPs, some can not hop

Some run so free
But others can't see

And some show no fear
While others can't hear

He is so fast, he's never late
She has trouble, just thinking straight

So, which little bunny would you rather be?
Can't hear, always late or totally free?
There's really no choice for you and for me.

Well their's is a life just like yours and like mine
But perhaps everything is not just so fine

So offer a hand if ever you see
A bunny that's not just like you or like me.

Doing The Giving
(a rap song)

Yo, one of the things that's so cool about live'n
is the feeling you get dude, doing the give'n.

Yes, give'n I say is an awesome way
to get something yourself on any old day.

When you're give'n you're get'n, this may be confuse'n
But try it you'll see, it's win'n not lose'n.

Now give'n can take, ya know, many a form
hand holding, or sharing, or just being warm.

A kind little smile that covers your face
Can help any other in our whole human race.

So try it right now, look around and take aim
if you're finding it hard, then make it a game.

Just do it, you'll see, I kid you not
The feeling you get, yo, will help you a lot.

Will help you a lot, yes, will help YOU a lot.

I want to thank everyone who has opened this book to let me share my thoughts with them. By reading my poetry and viewing my illustrations, I hope we have found some common ground and that I have been able to plant some seeds of joy, happiness and togetherness.

Taylor

Made in the USA
Monee, IL
19 January 2024